WOMEN ON THE WALL

Answering The Call

BY FRANCES L. BANKS

Copyright © 2014 by Frances L. Banks

Women On The Wall
Answering The Call
by Frances L. Banks

Printed in the United States of America

ISBN 9781498410120

All rights reserved solely by the author. The author guarantees all contents are original and do not infringe upon the legal rights of any other person or work. No part of this book may be reproduced in any form without the permission of the author. The views expressed in this book are not necessarily those of the publisher.

Scripture quotations taken from the King James Version (KJV) – public domain

www.xulonpress.com

DEDICATION

I dedicate this book to my Mother, Annie Ree Miles. Who has been my role model since the day I was born. Mom you have always been in my corner and always told me that I can do all things through Christ Jesus. Even when I wanted to give up and throw in the towel you have always assured me that the greater was coming. Mom you introduced me to Jesus and you not only told me that we should always pray but you showed me. You are my first blessing and the first manifestation of favor over my life. I truly thank God for giving me a great teacher and awesome women of God on this journey. I'm truly equipped to be about my Fathers Business because I saw you operate in such excellence in the field. Mom I thank you for your love, compassion and patience that you freely gave me my whole life. I also want to thank you for always letting your light shine and never hiding it. Mom I can only pray that I am half of what you are to me to.

Love You Mommy

ACKNOWLEDGEMENT

First in foremost I have to thank my Heavenly Father. In my darkest hour when I was hurt and broken he spoke to me and gave me this book. He told me that this was not just a book but a movement and the platform for my ministry. I have seen God do great things in my life since that day and I look forward to all he is going to do.

To my Dad Samuel Banks thanks for being my listening ear and sounding board. I truly appreciate our long conversation we have about The Lord. Thank you for your excitement when I told you about this book it really pushed me to complete it. I thank and love you very much.

TO TEAM ANNIE REE (MY SISTERS AND BROTHERS)

To my sister Khadene Robertson thank you for reading and re-reading this book for me. Your feedback really helped me with the confidence I needed to bring this book to reality. Love your positive spirit and I love how you always have my back. I pray that I'm everything for you that you are for me. I love you more than you may ever know.

To my sister Darnella Banks thank you so much for being my confidant and my cheerleader. I don't ever have to question whether or not you love me, you are always there for me. I truly do love you and excited to see you walk into your destiny. I know that God has great things in store for you. I pray that you know that I am always here for you to lean on.

To my sister Mona Lisa Adams. Thank you for inspiring me to be a strong woman. I truly look up to you, no matter what you deal with in life you always stand strong. You have never let anything break you and hold you down. No matter how many times you get knock down, you get right back up fighting. You are an anointed woman of God and I pray that I'm around to watch you walk into your destiny. I love and appreciate you.

To my sister Raphalena Adams thank you for your support in everything that I do in my life. Seeing me through your eyes make me want to be the person you hold me up to be. I love that you always stand up and fight for yourself no matter what. I try to be like that and stand up for what is right. I love and appreciate you.

To my little brother Samuel Banks, I thank you for always being excited for me and what I do. I know you have so much stored in you and I am excited to see what God does and have for you. I love you always.

ACKNOWLEDGEMENT

To my big brother Robert Adams. I thank you for always being a fighter and never giving up. I have taken that strength and used it in my own life. I pray that you will accept the call that God has over your life and become the great man of God you are called to be. I love you.

To my Pastor Richard L. Grate thank you for showing me every side of ministry. Thank you for showing me the struggle and how to endure it but not give up. I have learned so much while I traveled with you from church to church. I have seen the good, the bad and the ugly yet I have always seen the Grace of God in every instance. I love you and appreciate you. I wish nothing but blessing for you and the Praise Tabernacle Ministries and the Holy Ghost Deliverance Family.

To Pastor Christine Gorham I truly thank God that I grew up under your leadership. I watched you as I grew up and was always in awe of you. The anointing and power that was on you as you preached the word always held me captive. I could not take my eyes off of you while you preached. You operated in such authority and your spirit commanded respect. Everyone around you gave great respect: men, women, bishop, Apostle and teacher alike. Whatever struggle you went through I know nothing of it because you walked with such grace and love as if all was well. You are one of my biggest role models in ministry because I saw you stay on the wall and build and never getting tired. You lived in, operated in excellence, in righteousness and holiness. Thank you for always living what you preach. I will love you always.

I could not name all the people in my life that pushed me to become the womanI am today. I thank everyone that prayed for me and went before God on my behalf. I thank everyone who encouraged me and spoke blessing in my life. Thank you to everyone who saw the gift and anointing on my life and did not allow me to leave their sight without letting me know it. To everyone who I encountered and had a learning experience whether it was good, bad or indifferent I thank you because it made me stronger.

CONTENTS

I. INTRODUCTION xiii
II. A CALL TO THE BUILDERS 15
III. THE MANDATE TO WOMEN 17
IV. THE ISSUE OF THE PEOPLE 21
V. THE MISTREATMENT OF WOMEN IN MINISTRY 39
VI. YOU ARE RESPONSIBLE FOR YOUR PORTION
    OF THE WALL 43
VII. THE WALL WILL CHANGE YOUR LIFE 43
VIII. YOU MUST STAY ON THE WALL
    OR YOU WILL DIE 49
IX. GOD IS NOT A THIEF OR A ABUSIVE MAN 57
X. A MADE UP MIND 59
XI. WHEN QUITTING LOOKS GOOD 63
XII. PRAYER IS THE WAY OUT 67
XIII. INTERCESSORY PRAYER 71
XIV. ABOUT THE AUTHOR 75

I.
Introduction

Women On The Wall is a movement for the women of God to stand up and take their rightful place in the kingdom. It is a mandate for the women of the kingdom to fullfil what God has purposed and designed them for. Whether your calling is to be a preacher, teacher, evangelist, doctor, lawyer, author, usher, mother etc… whatever it is we must make sure that God gets the glory out of it. Women On The Wall is a vehicle to push women into their destiny and change their mindset from I can't to I can do all things through Christ Jesus who strengthens me. It is to make women aware that their lives are not by accident, but the father had a plan when he created you; His plan for you is to be blessed.

II.
The call to the builders

*I*n the book of Nehemiah the Bible says when Nehemiah heard about the state of his people he cried and prayed to God on their behalf. When I looked at the state of women in the kingdom of God it truly sent me to prayer. I see so many women in a state of wondering, trying to figure out their place. Some are so focused on becoming someone's wife and mother. There are also those who are so focused on proving their calling by God to others.

Women on the Wall is about Women standing up and completing their purpose. The kingdom of God is the responsibility of the Children of God (the sons and daughters) to build. We all have a part in the rebuilding of the wall which is the protection of the kingdom. Just as Nehemiah was given a mandate by God to rebuild the Walls of Jerusalem we have the mandate to rebuild the walls of the kingdom of God. The kingdom has gone through destruction just as it was in Jerusalem, the enemy has burned down the walls of the kingdom and now all kinds of mess has crept up in it. We have let the world dictate to us what is acceptable. The Kingdom is looking more and more like the world. We must take our place as the examples to the world to show them how they should be, yet it seems as if we have fashioned ourselves after them.

III.

The mandate to women

The Bible states Shallum the son of Halohesh the ruler of half of Jerusalem and his daughters put up their portion of the wall. This mean that there were women on the wall rebuilding for the kingdom (Nehemiah 3:12). Women have a determination to please their daddy, to make sure their father is proud of them. So when we put our mind to something there is no stopping us. So many women that are single mothers have worked gone to school after work, paid the bills took care of the kids and are now successful financially and spiritually. These women will tell you it was hard but something inside them would not let them quit. We have to be that same way with Gods business.

We women must fight through adversities. Whenever God places a purpose inside of you, you should fight for it like there is no tomorrow. The more people say you Can't do it that should make you want to turn up your fight even more. You should refuse to be anyones statistic. When you're a child of the King nobody should be able to put you in a box. You're not like other people who have been through similar situations and don't know Jesus. You should be clear that the way everybody else deals with their struggles is not the same way a King's kid deals with theirs. People can run all through your history if they like but they can never put a title on you that God himself has not given you.

Women of God do not fall apart and give up like other folks and die. Death is not your only way out of no way. When you're low you must remember you have a God that sits high. When you're scared you must remember your heavenly father has leagues of angels looking over you, ready to come to your rescue at any time. You don't have to worry about how you're going to make ends meet, because the world belongs to your father and the fullness there of (Psalm 24:1). That means everything you need, your Father owns it, and he loves to give to His children.

No matter what people may say or think about us we know that all things work together for our good for them that love God for those who are called according to His purpose (Romans 8:28). If you have purpose you have power and ain't no devil in hell or hater on earth can stop you from fulfilling your purpose. For that reason you must know who you are and what you are in God. You will only accomplish this by knowing that you are here for a purpose you must seek God to find out what is His purpose for you.

Please know that we all are responsible to build up the kingdom. The women must do their part to rebuild the wall just like the women in Nehemiah's day. If the ruler of half of Jerusalem did not put his daughters to work then a large portion of the wall would have been undone. Then the commission that God had put out would have come back to Him void. Women, simply put there are no excuses, we must do our due diligence to contribute to the rebuilding of the wall so that the kingdom of God can be established and the people of God can be blessed.

The kingdom needs all body parts to be working for it to function as God has predestined. Women must teach and preach the word. We must also show the love of Christ. The word says with love and kindness have I drawn you (Jeremiah 31:3).

We must look out for one another and not be in competition with each other. We must share knowledge with one another and build each other up, instead of tearing each other down. If you see something wrong with your sister don't gossip about her, try to understand her so you can positively help her. Don't attack your sister if her blessings are flowing, praise God for her blessing so you can know how to praise him when you receive your blessings.

IV.

The Issue Of The People

In the book of Nehemiah the report of the state of Jerusalem came back to Nehemiah and the report was not good. Nehemiah was informed that not only was the people in bad shape but the Kingdom was in ruins. When Nehemiah heard of this he was greatly grieved and straight away went to fasting and praying for his people and his kingdom. In return God gave him a mandate to go and rebuild the kingdom and the people of God. Whenever God is looking to make changes or establish a movement of God He sends someone to eye witness the issue. If you are never aware of a problem how can you be in a position to fix it. That's why they say the first step in recovery is admitting that you have a problem in the first place. In my travels with my Pastor we have visited many churches, God has always had me as an observer, paying close attention to what's going on around me. For some reason I am always drawn to the state of the women in the kingdom of God. I have seen things that have made me feel like Nehemiah which drove me to weep, fast and pray.

There is a disconnection in the kingdom concerning women, not only the action of women but the treatment of women as well. During this observation process I have seen diverse types of women in the churches that I can break down into five categories/subgroups. The Husband Seekers, The Anointed but feel Incomplete, The Misguided Young Women, The Insecure Wife and The Mothers of Judgment. It is not my position that every woman fit into these mold but there are far too many that do. I will try to describe these five different groups of women and I am sure that we all have someone who has these characteristics in our church.

The Husband Seekers

There are ***the women who are there only to find an husband.*** It's not about salvation for them it's clear that they are there to find their Boas. These women are constantly being taken advantage of, there are some men in church who are wolves in sheep clothing preying on these women. Since righteousness is not what these women thirst after they fall victim to these men all the time. These men use them sexually and after their done they move on to the next victim. When you speak with these women and ask why they allowed themselves to be used and taken advantage of? The excuse is always "I thought that he was my husband/Boas sent by God". When will we get that

God will only send us good and perfect gifts? I'm not saying that the men will be perfect because none of us are perfect but he will be perfect for you.

Women must stop lying on God and admit that it was their own lust that carried them away not a word from the Lord. Some of these women don't even take time out to spend with God to know the plan he has for them. These women desired then decided that they were going to make this man their husband, and it didn't work out that's why they are bitter and have the audacity to be upset with God. I know it's tight but its right they have free will, if they decide to play with lions and get devoured that's their fault. Nobody told them it was a house cat and its ok to go pet it. God gave them two eyes to see if they want to play blind that's on them. Pain doesn't need eyes and no matter how much these women try they cannot pretend the pain away.

The Bible says seek you first the kingdom of God and His righteousness and all these things shall be added unto you (Mathew 6:33). When you sincerely go after God and live a righteous life God will place the right person in your life. God does not desire for us to be alone he actually said " it is not good for man to be alone" (Genesis 2:18). God wants us to be happy, Jesus said "I come that you have life and have it more abundantly" (John 10:10). The Bible also says that He is a rewarder of those that diligently seek Him (Hebrews 11:6). When you seek after God whole heartedly not to pretend in order to catch the eye of a man or should I say

Boas. God will recognize your true praise, your true worship, your true love for him, and he will reward you with the desires of your heart. He knows you, your wants, needs and desires but you must wait on the Lord. Stop going out searching for your husband/Boas leaving yourself open to be taken advantage of. The Bible says he that finds a wife find a good thing not she that finds a husband/Boas (Proverbs 18:22).

The anointed but feel incomplete

The women who are anointed meaning have the power of God working through them. The oil is very defined in their lives and is poured out from their heads to their toes. Why do we as women think that we need a man to complete us? So many single women in the kingdom have such great anointing on their lives to do great things. These powerful women have such greatness in them and could make such an impact on the world. However, they feel like even with all these great things going on in their lives, they still become so consumed with the idea of being married. These women lose focus on the gift and mandate that God put on their life. I'm not saying that we should not want to be a wife, nor am I saying that God does not want you to be or desire to be a wife. Let me repeat it again In fact the word of God says it is not good for man to be alone, it also says that he that find a wife find a good thing. Now let's stay on this scripture for a minute.

The Bible says he finds a wife that means God does not expect us women to go and find a husband, however we are expected to be the women that he designed us to be. God is clear on the plans that he has for the men of God. The word says how could two walk together as one unless they agree (Amos 3:3). We must look at our lives as preparation for God to put us together to become the good thing. We as women should not feel like we need a man to complete us, we are who we are with or without a husband. But it is good to have a husband to complement who we are. When you're beautiful you're beautiful but makeup compliments your beauty. Your clothes just compliment you they don't make you. This is how we should feel about relationships, that they compliment who we are already.

There is no competition in God and everyone doesn't carry the same anointing. Women that means that your sisters are not your enemy, adversary or competitor. Never look to your sister and be envious of her anointing. If some of you knew what she had to go through to get that anointing some of you would run for the hills. Please understand what God has for you it's for you and no one can take that. You must remember that you can only be what God called you to be that is the best you. Don't sit and wish and desire to be like your sister because that's telling God what He planned for you is not good enough. Could you imagine telling a perfect God that his plan for your life is imperfect. Wow! that just hit me that when we reject God's plan for our lives, we are telling a perfect God that he has an imperfect plan.

I am who God says I am and I am happy with just that. God designed me he knows all my needs and wants. He also knows what is good for me and what's not. If we look at our lives and see how God has taken us through all the trials that we deal with, we would realize the very storm that we have in our lives is pushing us closer and closer to our Destiny. Some of us would have never tapped into our God giving gifts if we had not gone through a storm. When we go through a storm that is when we seek God like never before. That's when we pray and fast like never before. Now we are looking for an answer to our question why? We find ourselves asking God why am I going through this? For me when something hurts so badly I need a reason for my pain. I need to learn the lesson so that I can avoid repeating it.

Over the course of many years, I have realized when I am in the press that's when I can hear God clearly. When God needs your attention He is going to get it. That's because he has a set time for things to take place in your life. We as women sometimes get so wrapped up in things that we lose focus on mandates that God has placed on our lives. God being his wonderful self-sees us not at the mark in our time line of life. I say "ours" because God is not subjected to time. Just like they say he is an on time God. He intervened so that he can push us to hit the mark on time. You also have to be at the right place in your life at the right time to receive your blessings.

The Bible shows us this example over and over again. Moses had to be exiled from Egypt and end up on top of Mount Sinai so that God could speak to him and could use him to free his people. Esther had to end up with her uncle who gave her to be groomed to become a queen. Esther then becomes dependent on Hege the keeper of the women who then took a liken to her. He showed her everything she needed to do to get the eye of the king and she followed it to the letter. Esther became Queen and saved her people from death (see the book of Esther). There is a process and a time line God has for your life. It may seem like you're going nowhere. You may be lost right now but I promise you that once you hit the mark in your time line that's when the revelation is going to come. The instruction for your next step in life is there.

We cannot continue trying to rush through this life without instruction or some would say a road map. We need the master planner to give us clear instructions so that we won't make major mistakes or take so many detours in our life. Unfortunately we seem to only be great listeners after we have gone through something. That seems to be the time in our lives where God gets to push and we actually move in the right direction. Do what God is pushing you to do, don't focus on being single and wanting a husband, children, position or title. Don't be worried or frustrated because it has not happened yet, you just have not come to that point in your time line yet. Stop trying to go directly to the end of the book before you even read the story.

Have you ever thought that maybe you are not ready for the position/purpose or man that God is preparing for you. Even better the man is not yet ready for you. What if neither of you have reached the point in your lives where God has given the revelation on how to be a Godly husband/Godly wife. Maybe He has yet to give you the revelation on how to operate in your purpose and complete your commission. Maybe God is still teaching you how to be a Godly wife and virtuous women at the same time. This is no easy task but can be done. The Bible says while you're getting all your getting get understanding (Proverbs 4:7). There is an anointing that must come over your life to be able to handle all that God is going to place in your life. You must have the spirit of God to guide you into all truths or you will make a mess of your life. In order for you to succeed at this level you must be humble enough to consult the spirit of God about everything in your life. Simply you must be spirit lead completely.

The Misguided Young Women

There are ***the young women/ Youth*** in the church who are just lost. They do have a sincere heart and are truly looking for something. But too many are getting caught up with the sensation of church and falling short on the relationship with God. They know how to dance/shout like nobody's business they practice it at home as if they were going to do a step competition. There are so many of them who want to perform on the praise and worship team or in the choir.(Side note saints please let's get back to true praise and worship). I don't want to go to a concert every Sunday morning when I come into the house of the true and living God. Sometimes you been through so much hell all week long and when you make it to the house you need real praise, real worship there is such an urgency so much so you need to be in the presence of God or you just might lose your mind literally. The last thing you want to watch is a bunch of people show boating and trying to out riff each other.

This reminds me of something I witnessed one day I was in church and one of the singer's microphone went out and she stood there shaking her microphone at the sound people telling them to fix it and would not sing. I have seen preachers microphone go out and they would just keep on preaching until it came on. This girl had the nerve to stop singing. Let me say this just because you can sing does not mean that you are anointed.

There are some people who are talented and have a gift to sing, then there are people who are talented and gifted singers but are also anointed. You can always tell the difference between someone who is just talented or is truly anointed. Whenever you have an anointed person singin, the Spirit of God will move through the sanctuary in a powerfully way. I have seen folks get delivered and give their hearts to the Lord just by singing an anointed song. I have seen preachers who are not self-proclaimed singers (actually they confess that they are not singers at all), yet God will press a song upon their hearts and they will sing that song and the power of God will start moving. They are not trying to entertain the congregation by doing great riffs or vocal tricks, but because the anointing makes the difference it destroy every yoke. God can move in that kind of atmosphere and the people of God can be in the presence of God. You must realize that it's not about you but about God, you cannot steal Gods glory it does not belong to you.

Praise and worship is not your concert time, singing in the choir is not your concert time. That is not the time to show boat and make people notice you. It is the time where you are to sing about the goodness of our Lord and point people in His direction to give Him praise.

Young women let's stop all the clique business in the church. There should not be episodes of the Haves and the Haves Nots in the church. The ones who think they're beauty queens with the long weaves and the nice clothes and makeup all want to stick together. The singers want to stick together, the loose girls want to stick together, the ones who are trying to live right want to stick together and the list goes on. Every group is looking down on the other group yet everyone is claiming that they want to go to the same place, heaven. In heaven we will all be on one accord there will be no cliques there. We will all be together as sisters and brothers, showing love one to another. There will be no haves and haves not or the better then. If we all are to be like Christ and there is only one Christ then there can only be one clique. If you do not fit into the be like Jesus clique then you have to much work to do, work on being like Jesus, use that energy you have to dislike others on getting to know Jesus.

I think about the story of Mary and Martha the two sisters of Lazarus. When Jesus came to their house to visit, Martha was too busy running around trying to serve and making things perfect for everyone who was there. The question is, was she doing it out of the goodness of her heart or was she doing it for recognition? The Bible says when you do a good deed don't let your left hand know what your right hand is doing (Mathew 6:13). My mother told me whenever you do something from the heart that you shouldn't look for recognition you do it because that is what you desire. We know that Martha wanted it known what she had done because she went and told Jesus that she was doing everything and her sister would not help her. Now in those days if you were not married or if you're father was dead your oldest brother would have rule of you and the house. That means that Lazarus was the head of the household but Martha did not go tell Lazarus she told Jesus. My point of this shows that Martha was looking for recognition or glory for her hard work, but when she came to Jesus what she was looking for is not what she received. Jesus said Martha you are trouble and worried about a lot of things (see Luke 10:34).

Jesus did not glorify her for what she was doing but he did recognize Mary for what she was getting. That is what you young women must realize God is not impressed with your show he is excited about your heart. But if you be like Mary and grab hold to what she grab hold to like Jesus said it will never depart from you. You young women get on the choir, praise Worship team, usher board, youth leadership or whatever church clique you belong to that is not the thing that is important. Jesus said to Martha you are cumber about meaning you are running around doing a bunch of stuff but what Mary is doing she will be able to use it for her entire life and she will never lose it. What was Mary doing she was sitting at Jesus feet listening to his teaching capturing every word that came out of his mouth.

The Bible says that man shall not live by bread alone but by every word that come out of the mouth God (see Mathew 4:4). Martha was worried about the natural food that will only full you for a short amount of time, while Mary was after spiritual food that would sustain her for life. Mary put herself in a position of submission as she sat at His feet humbling herself to the Lord. Reverencing him knowing that she was in the presence of something greater than she had ever come across. She didn't care about whom else was in the building, she had her eye stayed on Jesus. She was not looking to be recognized or glorified she just wanted to be in his presence. She was forming a relationship with Jesus no one or nothing else mattered. That's how you should be young women forget everything else sit down at the feet of Jesus, learn of Him and His ways. Humble yourself so that you can feel his presence and his glory. You cannot make it without the bread of life and only Jesus can give it to you. Everything else you do will not last you can be sat down from the praise and worship team, choir, as a musician, usher board, youth leadership, and any other auxiliary by your Pastor. Your clique can decide they no longer click with you and kick you out. I have seen it happen on many occasions and the young women are absolutely broken hearted.

<u>The Insecure Wife</u>

To the married women you do not have to be so guarded at all times. I know there are women in the church who are pretenders and are waiting for that opportunity to make a move on your husband but that is not every single woman in the church. Every woman that smiles is not trying to catch the eye of your husband. When you put yourself in the position where you don't trust anyone you are allowing the spirit of fear to rule you. If you have the spirit of discernment you would be able to discern between whom is just showing the love of Christ from who is just full of lust. If you don't have discernment then you should do what the Bible says pray and ask the Father for it (Philippians 1: 9-10).

Please understand that everyone you hurt or offend you will have to answer for it. God is not going to accept the excuse of you were trying to protect your husband and that's the reason why you were bitter and nasty to someone. God knows who is after true friendship or even knowledge or understanding. You don't know who your assignment to teach is. Teaching could be your gift that God anointed you with, but you are allowing the spirit of fear to hold you back. The Bible says try the spirit by the spirit to see if it is of God (1 John 4:1). If you have the spirit of God you should be anointed enough to know if someone is truly reaching out to you or have a hidden agenda.

Stop being nasty to the young women who are pretty and well put together in church, because of your foolishness you run them right back out of the church even though they have not even spoken to your husband. You have allowed fear to grip you so tight that you even let the "what if " grasp you. What are the "what if's"? What if my husband is attracted to her?, What if she is attracted to him? What if they hook up and he leaves me and the kids? I have a question how much do you think of yourself? You must think very little of yourself to allow a total stranger, who you nor your husband know anything about come in and swoop your husband away. If you know something is wrong in your household then you should have already been working on that.

Where is the confidence that you should have knowing that you are the best thing that ever happened to him? Why is there no confidence that your husband is a true man of God and will live by God's Commandment? Do you not believe that the man truly love Jesus? Remember Jesus said if you love me keep my commandments (John 14:15). When you hold on to that bitterness and envy, jealousies, fear, discontent in your heart you will not grow spiritually and you won't receive the blessings that God has in store for you. Let me just go there, if you die with all that mess in your heart hell is where you will open your eyes. Please pray and ask God for discernment and use the spirit of discernment to see who have a right spirit.

Married Women stop judging other women by their appearance to place them in the "what if's" zone. Stop being nasty and bitter it is not necessary ever. No one is saying that you should be bff's with everyone but you should be able to show the love of Christ to all your sisters in Christ. Please keep in mind that married women also have affairs with other married women husbands. I notice that the married women like to form little cliques too. They all hang with each other because they figure she has her own husband she have no need for mine. Just because she has her own doesn't mean she is happy and not looking at yours. You have been running your mouth telling her all about the things he do to you and for you. She just might want to replace you.

To Mothers Of Judgement

I truly love each and every one of them, but I must say this they are not God so please stop judging. When women come to church whether they are young or old they are looking for guidance. They are looking for nurturing and wisdom, knowledge and understanding. Who better to lead them and guide them into a relationship with Christ than a mother figure, yet too often these women find themselves in the hands of an abusive mother who only wants to talk about how they don't dress right or how they don't speak right and even how they're not living right. Well they know all of that and much more that's why they're in the church in the first place.

The Bible says that the older women are to teach the younger women (Titus 2:4). How can these Mothers teach someone that they have alienated and made feel as though they were less than nothing. These Mother's talk about the way they give God praise talking about "she's faking it or it don't take all that".

These Mother's have no idea what these women have been through in their lives. There are women whom have been molested by their mother, father, sister, brother, uncle, aunts, friend of the family and the list continues. There are women whose parents sold them for drugs when they were little girls too innocent to comprehend the ills of the world. There are women whom have been abused by boyfriends, husbands mentally, emotionally or physically sometimes all the above. Women who have low self-esteem who believe that they are nothing and worth nothing. These women have gone through some stuff, oh yeah "it takes all that" and then some for them. I know that there are some that come and play church but I think about the story Shirley Caesar told about how she used to play church until one day God or in her words "something got a hold of me" and she wasn't playing anymore. Just because someone is not where you think they're suppose to be does that mean we turn our back on them? I'm going to say it like the Apostle Paul said it " God Forbid".

Mothers you have the knowledge and the wisdom that women seek. Give the knowledge and wisdom without the judgment. Jesus said with love and kindness have I drawn you. When you give correction and you should give it, you must know how to give it with love and kindness. Don't come off as holier then thou because everyone has fallen short of the glory of God. Don't talk about the women instead pray for them that God will renew their minds. When women come to you in confidence don't gossip to the other mothers about them because somehow the word always get out and you hurt the women you were suppose to help. Now this woman has turned away from God because of church hurt, mother you are responsible for that and God will make you pay.

I must say this just because you are an older woman and respected as mother of the church, it does not give you the right to say whatever you want to the younger women stop talking about women's weight, nobody asked you. Stop talking about the women's clothing, nobody asked you. I have come to the realization that these older women seem to always have issues or concerns about the way women are dressed particularly the young women. I heard a phrase that I really liked, "before you can clean a fish you have to catch it". That means focus on their souls not there clothes.

When I first started out in church my clothes were a little tight fitting, short, and my shirts maybe a little low cut but when I really formed a relationship with Christ and received the Holy Ghost everything changed. Nobody had to tell me anything; one day I put on a dress that I had worn many times before but that particular day the spirit spoke to me and told me to change that dress. I first thought to myself for what I worn this dress plenty times before. I started to keep the dress on, but then such a conviction came upon me that I could not keep it on, I went and changed right away. Ever since then everything that the spirit convicts me of I would straight away change. I am telling you that the Holy Spirit will guide you into all truth. I say that to say let these women receive the Holy Spirit and let Him change them. Mothers you help lead them to a relationship with Jesus Christ and he will do the rest.

V.
The Mistreatment of Women in Ministry

I never understood why women in ministry must go through so many obstacles to prove that God called them to ministry. If we preach hard then we trying to be like a man, if we preach soft then we are not anointed. I need to understand when did God give man the right to delegate who He can call to do His work. God can and will call who every he wish to work in his kingdom. I find it really strange that the same pastor who ordained you will be the same person who will hold you back. Why is it okay for women to lead prayer, teach bible school, Sunday school, but seemingly cannot expound upon the word Sunday morning, that same anointing women use to pray and teach women can use that same anointing to bring forth the word.

Women should not be limited to platform services and women services. If God put a word in our mouth and revelation of his word in our heart who has a right to stop that. Women in ministry should be treated no different than men in ministry. God does not require women in ministry to be on television, preach to thousands at conferences or grace high profile platforms to be acknowledged as anointed women of God. The bar should not be held so high for women and the bar for men in ministry be almost nonexistent . I recall when I became licensed as a minister along with two other women and three men. We visited a church after we were licensed and the pastor of the church made an announcement that the men were just licensed and he invited them to the pulpit. The thing that got me is just like he heard the men were just license I know he knew that the women were also, yet he chose not to even acknowledge the women nor did he invite us to the pulpit. This Pastor does not acknowledge women in ministry which I find pretty ridiculous that he feels he has more authority than God. There are many men who are hung up on the scripture that a man has rule over his wife. That is biblical and I accept that statement that the husband is the head over his household and Christ is the head of all. Let's be very clear that is the relationship between a husband and wife. This scripture does not state that men have rule over all women. I have not read nor have I seen it written that there is any superiority giving to men in general Jesus is the perfect one not men or women.

I recall having a discussion with a young man about poor choices he was making and laying out clear references about how his choices were affecting and hurting the ministry. This young man became very upset and had the nerve to tell me that I should be quiet and be obedient to him like the Bible says. I chuckled a little bit at his ignorance and then made him aware that I am not subjected to be obedient to him because he clearly was not my husband. If anyone was out of order biblically it clearly was him because the Bible does state respect your elders and I was in the elder position, since he wanted to be textual that night. The sad thing about it is that someone had provided this young man with misinformation, that has now been trickled down to another generation. That means the women of God of that generation will also have to endure the fiery darts and the trials and hardship we women of God have to face today.

Jesus didn't come the way people expected Him to come ,that's why the Pharisees denounced Him. Even though Jesus performed many miracles he healed the sick, raised the dead, yet they still did not believe that he was the savior that all the prophets talked about. Women we must be like Jesus no matter what obstacles he endured he kept on going. Jesus was on this earth to do His father's business he gave no care for himself. Even when they threatened to kill him and beat him it didn't matter, Jesus knew what he was on this earth for. You also must be willing to go through all the persecution, disrespect, mistreatment and being overlooked. These struggles should be light afflictions, remember Jesus after he went through all his trials and tribulation and even death he still got the victory and all power was in his hands. Jesus was victorious because he refused to give up. Women will experience that level of triumphant in ministry if we just don't give up.

The Bible says if we want to reign with Christ we first have to suffer with Christ. Everyone didn't follow Jesus he was not effective everywhere he went the Bible said not even in his own town where he grow up. There were people who just didn't accept that He was the savior the Bible says that he could not do great miracles because of the people's disbelief . Jesus even said that a prophet gets no reward in his own home. We must always remember Jesus' words "I didn't come to preach to the righteous nor to the healthy but to the sick the lost sheep and the lonely at heart". Women please remember that we are not here to debate with any doctrine or ideology, but God called us to preach the good news. Women preach to the lost sheep, preach to the sick, preach to the ones in bondage, preach until the captives are set free. Let the world know that you are about your fathers business. Keep your heart and your mind stayed on Jesus and he will keep you in perfect peace. No matter what attacks you go through remembering no weapon formed against you shall prosper. No deadly thing can touch you, you will tread upon serpents. Everything that will try to keep you out of the will of God shall be trampled under your feet.

VI.

You are Responsible for your Portion of the Wall

The kingdom of God is made up of many. Jesus said the kingdom of God is neither here nor there but the kingdom of God is in you (Luke 17:21). Therefore we all are responsible for the kingdom and the walls to protect it. The mandate is to all in the kingdom to rebuild what has been destroyed. We should all have an urge and a desire to get everything out of place in the kingdom back in order. The Bible says the kingdom suffers violence but the violence take it by force (Mathew 11:12). This scripture rains truth, the kingdom has and is suffering much violence. There are so many different things going on in the church that are damaging the kingdom. We have become so focus on prosperity and fame. So many women go to church just to find a husband whether they belong to somebody else or not. The church or should I say the kingdom has now been opened up to so much mess that now the walls are in ruins. The very foundation has been shaking. There are so many different doctrine today that it makes you ask the question how many Jesus' are there? Every denomination have their own doctrine and revelation from God and none of them line up with each other.

My God is not a God of split personality the Bible says he is the same yesterday, today and forever more. The Bible also says that He is not the God of confusion (1 Corinthians 14:33) so I have to ask the question who is speaking in these churches that so many are teaching so differently? The alter calls for salvation are slowly dwindling. I've seen more people run to the altar for a thirty (30) day blessing than to be healed or saved. The sad thing is that they don't realize if you're not whole you will not be truly able to enjoy the blessings. They want God to bless them with their own house but they don't have a job and can't keep one. Some people want God to bless them with a car but they don't have a driver's license. Some want God to bless them with a raise or just more money but they don't pay their bills or tithes. So many women want God to bless them with a husband but they still have hurt and unforgivness in their heart. Whatever is in them at some point will spill out and cause great stress which can lead to their losing everything. God does not want you to lose what He's blessed you with. What God does in the midst of your frustration is try to point out to you, your need to accomplish something. That something is your purpose your contribution to the building up/rebuilding of the kingdom and the walls to protect it.

Nehemiah was the cupbearer for king Xerxes, he had favor within the king's and queen's sight. He was living a pretty good life but when he heard about the people of God and the kingdom. He no longer thought about self his purpose and his call leapt up so much in him that all he could do is cry out to God. He could not eat nor sleep, the Bible said that he was so unhappy that right away when the king and queen saw him they knew something was wrong. The Bible also makes mention that the King and Queen had never seen him unhappy (Nehemiah 2:2). We have to really be focused and understand where our unhappiness and even depression is coming from. As women we always assume that it's something going on in our personal life. If we're single we believe it's because we do not have a husband. We trick ourselves to believe that if we had a husband all the sadness and depression will be gone. If we are not yet mothers we make ourselves believe that having a child will make it all better. The married women believe they are dealing with sadness or depression because their husbands are not spending enough time with them or showing them enough love but this is the trick of the enemy. Have you ever thought that maybe just maybe we deal with sadness and depression because we are feeling the hurt of God? Maybe he is saying you're not spending enough time with Him or you're not doing your chores as I your father have commanded you to do. Jesus said that greater works shall you do because he was going to the father (John 14:12). So who is responsible to build up/

rebuild the kingdom? It is our responsibility, the people of God to get the kingdom of God ready for his return.

Men and women must be on the wall rebuilding as they did in Nehemiah's day. When we are disobedient to God we don't feel like ourselves, the Bible says seek ye the kingdom of God and all his righteousness and all these thing shall be added unto you. It also says in the presence of the Lord there is the fullness of joy (Psalm 16:11). When you're about your father's business you have no choice but to be in his presence therefore there will be great joy in your life. No matter what situation or circumstances your dealing with. When you experience great trials, hurt and storms if you're on the wall building/ rebuilding the kingdom, God will make sure you come out whole and on top. God said if you are faithful over a few things he will make you ruler over all (Mathew 25:23). When you take care of Gods business he will take care of your life, your spirit, and replenish your soul.

When you keep your eye on God you're not focused on what's going on around you. Yes you see it, you're aware of it, you will not be ignorant to the fact but it cannot harm you, break you or better it cannot stop you. When you're in the will of God He will bless you greatly. If you're waiting on something that God promised you, work while you wait, for while you're busy working the wait time doesn't seem that long. Have you ever been at work having a crazy day and the next thing you look up and it's almost time to go home that's what it's like when you get busy in the kingdom before you know it everything that God promised you, you will receive it. It is so important for us women to be on the wall rebuilding. because all the things we deal with as women would be such a lighter load for us. When we are working we ain't got time to give in to our extreme emotional moments that we have as women. It's nothing to be ashamed of that is a part of our genetic makeup. God knows how we were created because he created us.

The Bible says there is nothing that have taken you unknown to man but God is faithful he gives you a way of escape (1 Corinthians 10:13). Although we are emotional beings God knows that we are driven and when we focus on a task there is nothing that will stop us. I have seen women relentlessly go after something whether it be a man, job, having a child, car, promotion or to hate or discredit or attack someones character. They're driven to complete or accomplish what they've conceived in their minds to do in the end they achieved what they set out to do.

VII.

The Wall Will Change your Life

When Nehemiah accepted his assignment from God his life changed completely. When you obey God He will take you to places you've never thought you would go. The things that you tried to do when you were disobedient to the Lord and did not acknowledge Him it never seemed to work out. Those very same things become an easy task when you're in the will of God. God is a rewarder of them who diligently seek after him. Just like Nehemiah, God will put you in the position of authority when you're on the wall. You will be able to speak a thing and it shall happen. He will make you the head and not the tail (Deuteronomy 28:13). The doors will be open that you never had access to before you will find that you have favor in everything that you do. The best part of it all, is knowing that you are pleasing in God's sight things will be set in order.

We must look closely at the moves that Nehemiah made. He didn't just make sure the wall was rebuilt he made sure that order was reestablished in Jerusalem. Nehemiah had it so everyone gave their tithes so there would be no lack. He made sure the Levites were put back in place so that the services of God were brought back to order. Nehemiah also reinstated and made certain that the the Sabbath was being observed. He also declared that no outsiders could come into the gate on the Sabbath to disrespect their God. Things in our lives will have to start lining up with what God requires when we are on the wall. God should always be first in our lives we should be trying to hit the mark of the high calling of God at all times. As we grow we should be getting closer and closer to our target.

The word says that everything should be done in decency and in order (1 Corinthians 14:40). God is a God of order not confusion; if your life is filled with confusion and you have no order whatsoever you need to get back on the wall because you have a lot of work and rebuilding to do. Remember Jesus said whatever you sow that shall you reap (Galatians 6:7). When you sow in confusion you reap confusion. But when you sow in order you will reap it. Nehemiah made sure he put God's business in order first, then he took care of the people. When you are on the wall your relationship with God is set in order first, then will your knowledge and understanding of what God has for you or should I say purpose for you is put in order. Then the blessing of God will rain down on you because you are in his will. When your life is in order your no longer wandering around saying what am I here for what is my purpose. God has already shared his plans with you and is showing up mightily in your life.

After your life is in order, you must take that next step like Nehemiah and help make provision for others in the kingdom. Jesus said the way that you know you are one of my disciples is that you show love one to another (John 13:34). When Peter and the disciples came to Jesus and asked which one of them would be the greatest. Jesus just basically said "the one who would be a server to the rest will be the greatest" (Mathew 23:11). We are expected to serve the kingdom of God. While you are busy working on the wall reach down and pull your sister up so that she can start her journey. I never understood why women are so "catty". Why do we think it's alright for us to fight against one another. If a woman feels good about herself and take pride in putting herself together women start talking about she think she is all of that or that she think she is better than the rest. God will give you beauty for ashes you don't know what trials and storms that woman has been through to get where she is today. I would give God praise when I see women whose lives are in order and the ones who are successful and at the top of their game. If you change your mind set and look at it like God did it for her he will do it for me. God has no respecter of person, He wants nothing but good for his children. As a child of God you have access just like every other child. There is no reason for us to be jealous of one another because all we have to do is get into the will of our father and he will pour out a blessing that you will not have room to receive.

VIII.

You Must Stay on the Wall or You Will Die

*L*ike Nehemiah you must not come down off the wall no matter what situation or destruction comes your way. Nehemiah knew that there was a plot to kill him, to prohibit the completion of the wall (Nehemiah 8:14). Please understand that the enemy does not want you to be on the wall in order to complete your assignment. He will do everything in his power to distract you so that you can lose focus. Have you ever notice that when you become so focused on God and growing spiritually that's when all hell seems to break loose around you. The moment you stop focusing on your relationship with God you start to feel like you are losing control, you start questioning God because you feel as if He has forsaken you, but the reality is you have forsaken him. When you stay connected to God He gives you the peace that surpasses all understanding.

When you stay focus on the situation it doesn't get better it just gets bigger. It's bigger because you are allowing it to consume you, all of your energy is thrown into it. It begins to take over your vision and even though the issue has not changed, your sight has increased it and now it's magnified a thousand times. When I look at my own life, every time I became focused on my issues and did not leave it in God's hands, everything fell apart. I remember when I was in college and I had an exam that I had to pass before I could graduate. I studied so hard for that exam I was stressing out because I was to graduate the next month. Usually I would study then pray and ask God to get me through it but this time I didn't. I was really nervous because it was a hard subject for me. I Stressed myself out so bad that I failed the test. I walked away from college for a little while. I felt so discouraged and defeated. After a while I decided to go back and finish what I started. This time I went to God first I prayed and had a conversation with Him, I was like " Lord you see what I am trying to do, Lord I cannot do it without you please help me". I took the exam again and passed with flying colors. This among other reasons are how I know that if you put God in every situation in your life whether big or small God will work it out for you.

The Bible says you receive not because you ask not (James 4:3). When you're on the wall don't come down for nothing. Your answer, your solution, your healing, your blessing, your way out of no way is right there on the wall with you, all you will need to do is ask. He will bring you out He will fix your problem no matter how rough your situation looks God specializes in miracles. If you just trust Him and believe that He is not a man that He should lie.

Nehemiah knew that as long as he was busy doing God's business on the wall no one could harm him, even though they were plotting to kill him. Please know that the enemy is plotting daily to kill you he will do everything possible to get your attention to get you off your wall. As Nehemiah did you better tell that devil I'm busy doing my father's work and I cannot come. Just know when you're serious about God's business He will take care of your business.

IX.
God is Not a Thief or Abusive Man

God is a powerful God he is all knowing and all seeing but he is not forceful. When God created us he gave us free will which means you can come to Him or not. The Bible says behold I lay before you life or death I suggest you choose life (Deuteronomy 30:19). The point that I am trying to make is that the choice is up to you. God is a gentleman he will never force you to serve him. Jesus said I stand at the door and knock and if you let me in I will come and sup with you (Revelation 3:20). It must be your choice to accept Jesus Christ as your Lord and Savior, after which you must get on the wall and get busy for God. You cannot continue to be in sin and call your self-working for kingdom. The Bible says who which you serve that is your master you cannot serve God and sin at the same time (Mathew 6:24).

There are so many people who live that double life they sing and work in ministry on Sunday and they are full of hell on Monday through Saturday and then they wonder why they are not being blessed. Be not deceived God is not mocked whatever a man sow that shall he reap. You cannot fool God the Bible says that a shepherd knows his sheep and his sheep knows his voice (John 10:27). You cannot pretend to be on the wall or half on and half off you have to be completely committed to the work that God has for you to receive the blessing. He is a rewarder of those who diligently seek after him you have to be totally sold out for God. Your motto must be for God I live and for God I die. When you get to that point in your life, when you really mean it, that's when you will start to see the changes in your life. That's when the blessing come pouring down on you and you can truly say If it had not been for the Lord on my side I don't know where would I be.

When you follow after God and do His will then and only then will you experience unspeakable joy and you can truly say this joy I have the world didn't give it to me and the world cannot take it away. No husband nor child can give you this kind of joy. Often times, that's what we look for to complete us, however we end up being miserable because we still feel so incomplete/deficient. We blame our current condition on the man he is not treating me right, he doesn't do this and he doesn't do that. The man is confused and saying something is wrong with this woman I can never please her. We sometime complain about the children, we grumble about how they won't behave, they are causing undue stress, whining saying I cannot handle it or I am so unhappy. The reality is that some of us did not seek after God for that unspeakable joy. Nobody but God can give you that kind of joy no matter what they do.

X.
A Made up Mind

The wall requires a made up mind. That is the qualification to work in our Father's business. The Bible says anyone who put their hands to the plow and turn back is not fit for the kingdom (Luke 9:62). When you make the decision to do the will of God you must be all in. The moment you make the decision the enemy will be hot on your trail. His job is to stop you from reaching your destiny. The enemy uses fear and confusion to deter you from your work. He battles you in your mind to push you out of your destiny.

I remember when I was really young I knew God had a calling on my life but the enemy would tell me that, what God wanted me to do was too big for me. He told me I would see and fight demons, that scared me, can you imagine telling the young you about demons, the thought alone sent me running for the rafters. I thought to myself there is no way on God's green earth I was going to fight demons and I absolutely did not want to see any demons, ain't nobody got time for that. So I ran from God because I allowed the enemy to overtake me with fear. This is a trick of the devil whenever he battles you, he makes you see things through his mind, he will tell you part truth and part lie. He has been doing this throughout the history, he told Eve surely you will not die if you eat the fruit and that was a lie and the truth at the same time. Eve would not die naturally which is what she thought or understood but she did die spiritually. The enemy is not going to tell you after you lose everything God is going to give you double for your trouble like he did Job. Just like the enemy didn't tell me that God did not give me the spirit of fear but of love, power and a sound mind (2 Timothy 1:7). He didn't tell me that after I receive the Holy Ghost that I will receive power and every demon is subjected to me and all I have to do is speak the word and call on the name of Jesus and demons must flee.

It is imperative for you to have a made up mind when you get on the wall because the storms will come, pain will come, hurt will come trouble will come; your unreserved stance ought to be "God I live and for God I die" nothing but what you do for God will last. When you say God have your way in my life that means you are giving him full control of your life. When you say I surrender all you really have to give him all.

This race is not for the swift or the strong but the one who endures to the end (see Ecclesiastes 9:11). When you have a made up mind nothing can detour you from your destination. You become so focus on your purpose that you don't even let self get in the way.

A Made up Mind

When your mind is made-up it doesn't matter if you have to go by yourself, you're going to make it to your destiny. If mommy doesn't go, if daddy doesn't go, you have to go full speed ahead. If I have to go with tears falling from my eyes if I have to go wounded I will put a bandage on it and keep going until I get there. If my money acting funny I will still go. If I don't understand as long as God is holding my hand I will go. No matter how many valley days I have no matter how dark it gets. I will not come down off the wall, I will finish the work.

Nehemiah received all kinds of threatening messages from his enemies, yet he would not come down from the wall. The messages kept coming the threats were real and he knew if his enemies had the opportunity they would kill him but he stayed on the wall to conclude his assignment. Nehemiah's rivals threatened him and the very people who he was working so hard to protect. Don't you know that if the enemy cannot get to you, he will go after the people you love? You have to know that it is only another attack from the adversary. Nehemiah kept on working but he made sure they were equipped and ready for battle in the event the need arose. The people worked on the wall with their weapons on one side and their tools on the other (Nehemiah 4:13).

Your praise and your prayers are your weapons, use them, for the weapons of warfare are not carnal but are mighty through God to the pulling down of strong holds (2 Corinthians 10:4). You must keep your weapons locked and loaded-at all times and don't anyone come down from the wall to fight the enemy. You can use your weapon of mass destruction right from where you are. Your weapons can kill your enemy no matter how close or how far he hides or take cover. You must know that God will take care of every situation and every circumstance that presents itself to you. Your focus is to complete the work that God has assigned to you.

XI.

When Quitting Looks Good.

There are times in your life when the road gets so rough and you feel like you just cannot breathe. When everything that could go wrong has. You have your heart broken and stepped on. Your heart is in pieces and you cannot stop the tears from flowing and you feel that at any minute you will just break. All you want to do is crawl up into yourself if possible and hide. There are times when you cannot even talk yourself through it or anybody else. When all you can say to God is why God why. When people are talking about you behind your back. When you walk in a room and half of the people hate you for no reason, when the very people you try to help scandalize your name, you must have a heart for the work.

There will be great trials and troubles that you will have to endure when you are working on the wall. That is why you have to have a heart for the work if you are doing the work for acknowledgement or to be appreciated by man you will not be able to endure to the end. If you need folks to love you and adore you, you will not make it. When you are doing the work for any other reason other than wanting to be about the fathers business you will be over your head. The work of the kingdom is a lonely road and a journey that is mostly singly traveled. No one but God will reward you for the work you do in the kingdom.

There is a process that we all must go through and the truth is, sometimes that process is a hard one. Sometimes you are put in a position where you give your everything and the very people who you try to help hurt you. In leadership there are some blows that you will receive that will shake you to your very core. Everything in you just want to give up and walk away you feel like no one understands what you're going through. It seems like everyone one has an opinion on what you should do with your life, then you go to God and the only answer you will receive is a simple my grace is sufficient for you.

Church hurt is the worse hurt and all you want to do is get away but God doesn't allow you to, why is that? Simply put, because he still has work for you to do. If you don't have the heart for God and want to have His will to be done, you will give up and throw in the towel. But, when you know it is about the greater and that you are living to live again, you recognize that all things are working towards your good, that the steps of a good man or woman is ordered by the Lord. You may cry and you may weep but you don't take down.

What can separate us from the love of God, not trials nor sickness (Romans 8:35).

You must see yourself at the end of your storm and know that victory is at the end. When you say for God I live and for God I die you must mean it. The race is not for the faint at heart nor for the swift or the strong. God is not concerned about the way you go through the storms he is concerned that you go through it. There will be times when you feel like giving up. I remember when I experience a great church hurt it was so extreme because it came from the top. On top of that I felt alone because none of the other leaders came to my defense, yet I understood why, no one wants to go against the head of the church, yet it added on to the hurt.

I remember just sobbing because I could not believe what had taken place I felt so disrespected and disregarded by this leader and to make matters worse, what devastated me was though this leader knew they had hurt me they refused to apologize. This leader did not want to make me whole even though the Bible states if you offend your brother/sister you must leave your offering at the alter and go get it right (Mathew 5:21-24). This taught me to never allow your expectation of people in leadership to hijack your heart for God, always remember that man has free will even the ones who claims to be of God. You must understand that even the ones who have the Holy Ghost can be guilty of offending. Just because someone is a leader in ministry they don't lose their free will they can decide not to be Obedient to the spirit of God.

God has to be able to trust you to stay on the wall no matter what issue or situation that you go throw. If you look at Nehemiah you will see that he went through great trials not only from his enemies but also from his own people. There was war in the camp among the very people he was trying to uplift, but because Nehemiah had a heart for the work God gave him, he didn't let anything or anyone stop the work.

XII.

Prayer is the Way Out

When Nehemiah heard about the plot of Sam Ballot to kill all Jews that were working on the wall, the Bible says Nehemiah began to pray. Nehemiah knew that the threats from his enemies were real and the truth of the matter was that if his enemies wanted to destroy him, the Jews, and the wall they were working on, they could have. Nehemiah knew that he served a God that sits high and looks low and when he called on him he would come to his rescue. As a Women of God when stuff starts hitting the fan prayer should be your knee-jerk reaction. Just like when you're driving and you see someone stop short in front of you, your knee-jerk reaction is to apply the brakes. Or when something is coming at you your knee-jerk reaction is to put your hands up for protection. That's how we should be about prayer. Prayer is communion with God, our time to go to father and make our request known. The Bible says man should always pray and pray without stopping (1

Thessalonians 5:17) Why do you think that is? The Bible also says you receive not because you ask not. If you ask God and it's in his will you will receive in due time if you faint not.

I always wonder why my mother's answer to everything while I was growing up was pray about it. I used to get so frustrated with her because every answer to my question was pray and ask God. I remember coming to her and asking about a relationship I was in and wondering if I should walk away from it. She was not fond of him and she could have easily said what she always said "I don't think he is the right person for you". Instead, her response was pray and ask God. God did confirm what she had been saying all along when I prayed I did get my answer. When I went to job interviews and I would really want the position I would come to my mother saying mom" I really want this job" my mother would always say let's pray about. Every question that I asked the answer would be pray. One day I had to ask "mom why is your answer to everything, to pray?" Her answer changed my life she said three (3) simple words "Because It Works" my mother was absolutely right prayer does in fact work.

I can think of countless times when my back was against the wall and my only remedy was prayer. Prayer becomes whatever you need in this life, if it is sickness your dealing with prayer becomes your healing. If it is deliverance you are in need of, prayer becomes your deliverance. If you are having money problems prayer becomes your money solver. Prayer fixes marital problems and put them back together. Prayer can make a non-believing husband become a believer. Prayer can put food on the table, clothes on your back, shoes on your feet. Prayer can make your kids act right and do well in school. Prayer can bring your sons out of jail and your daughters off the streets. Prayer can hang college degrees on your wall with 3.0 and higher GPA. Prayer can change the whole atmosphere on your job when folks are just acting crazy. Prayer will make the people that despise you bless you. I am talking about prayer that will change doctors reports and leave them scratching their heads. Prayer that will turn depression to unspeakable joy. Prayer is the gate way out of whatever situation or circumstance you are dealing with.

When we look at Jesus' life we see that Jesus prayed continually. Jesus the son of God knew that while He was on earth all the answers were in heaven. He went to the Father continually about every situation even about his death. Please remember that the answers to life issues are in heaven. That's why Jesus said when you pray you ask the father to let his will be done on earth as it is in heaven (Mathew 6:10) keep on praying until everything in your life that is not lining up to the will of God get in line.

Women this is our season to move with the power of God like never before. We must study the word and seek through the scriptures for new revelation. The Bible says that in the last days God is going to pour out his spirit. Women lets be available to receive the spirit of God like we have never done before. We are truly in the last and evil days, the great falling already has started if we women would get on the wall and build up our portion I believe the kingdom will get inline and God will do many miracles through his people. Women please don't let our Father come back and our work is undone. Get busy with our father's business put in the work, walk into your calling and destiny. When you have your eyes on your purpose, running towards your destiny, nothing and I do mean nothing can stop you. Get on the wall women and Don't Come Down!

XIII.

Intercessory Prayer

God I come to the throne of grace at this time for all the women who will read this book that you gave me. God you know that these are your words and your message to the women of God. I ask that you allow these words to penetrate their hearts and renew their minds. Father give them a hunger like never before, to seek your face and learn of your ways. Let them know that they can do all things through Christ Jesus that strengthen them. Lord let them know that every situation and every circumstance that they are going through shall pass. Let them know that weeping may endure for the night but joy is coming in the morning. Let your daughters know that no matter what it looks like, you are working on their behalf and they will come out victorious. Let the women know that the joy of The Lord is their strength Father, remind them that only what they do for you, God will last. Remind them to seek you and all your righteousness that all things will be added to them.

Father I pray that every woman will get busy with kingdom business and get on the wall and start laying kingdom bricks. For there is great work that needs to be done and God you expect all your children to do their part. God I pray that, a yes Lord ring out through all the women in the kingdom. Let there be a yes in every city, every state, Lord let there be an international yes God. A yes in the United States, the United Kingdom, Africa, the Caribbean. God let there be a yes in all nations every nationality and every race. Not just a simple yes but an absolute yes, a resounding yes, a working yes, a faith yes, a true yes. A yes that move mountains, a yes that kicks fear in the face, a yes that says I'm not sure what I am doing but never the less am going on. A yes that says if mommy doesn't go, if daddy doesn't go if brothers and sisters don't go, if my spouse doesn't go, friends don't go I still say yes God.

God I bind up the enemy who will come in and try to steal away their joy and their peace. We bind up fear and the spirit of hold back. Lord we know that you did not give us the spirit of fear but of love, power and a sound mind. We plead the blood of Jesus right now on every distracting spirit, every spirit of confusion and less than spirit in the name of Jesus. Father empower all the women of God to go forth in power, in spirit and truth. God I pray for the women who don't know you yet and read this book that the seed that is planted in them be sown in good ground. God do not allow the enemy to snatch it away from them, but let the seed spring up great and mighty. God use them for your glory. Lord I thank you and I praise you right now. I know that it is already done. So I give you the honor, I give you the glory and I give you the praise in Jesus' name I pray.

AMEN

XIV.
ABOUT THE AUTHOR

Frances L. Banks was born on December 20 in Staten Island, New York to Samuel Banks and Annie Ree Banks. Frances L. Banks Grew up with her sisters and brothers. At a very young age she knew that God had a calling on her life but was never really sure what it was. The one thing in her life that stood out was the fact that she had a passion to serve.

At a very young age she started to help the elderly whether it be helping them clean house or run errands, or just sitting and talking, she would serve in any way she was needed. As a child writing was always her first love she would write songs, poems, plays, and short stories. The empty pages of a notebook was her playground, she could create whatever story she liked and what was most exciting was that she could dictate how the story ended. She even won an award in college for writing an essay about her mother, who is the strongest woman she knows.

Frances decided that she would become a writer or a lawyer so, she acquired her Associates Degree in paralegal studies and then received her Bachelors Degree with a double major in political science and English literature from Hebert H Lehman College. However, God had different plans for her; because she found herself working for a union serving workers and fighting for their rights. This was an easy transition for her because she has been a sever all her life.

Francis always knew God had a plan for her life, although at times she wasn't sure what it was. However, God being who he is slowly revealed his plan to her, the gift of ministry. Her gift was not just the spoken word but also the written word. Afterwards, she worked and served as part of the leadership in her church. In 2013, she was officially licensed as a minister.

Frances L. Banks is a true anointed women of God who can preach and teach in power and authority. The oil is saturated in her life and now God is placing her in the position to reach out to the women in the kingdom to be a light and bring them to a closer relationship with God. Frances leads by example because what she preach she lives. She has a heart for people and is on a mission to uplift and push the men and women of God. Frances lives her life with the mindset that only what she does for God will last. This book is just the beginning of what God is going to do through this young woman of God.

I pray it blesses you.